Parents' Poetry

by Judy Theobald

Design: Life Publications Limited

First published Copyright © 2000 Life Publications Limited, 88 Newland, LINCOLN LN1 1YA.

Acknowledgements: Howard Spindley, Illustrations.
                         David & Sylvia Hughes, Illustration scanning.
                         Jo Clarke, Illustrations advisor.

Printed in Great Britain by: Meltons Printers of Lincoln,
                               Telephone 01522 541827.

A catalogue record for this book is available from the British Library.

ISBN 0-9506314-2-6

Dedicated to
Matthew and Sophie

Coupled with the memory of
Canon Mgr. Chris Fisher

CONTENTS

The Catholic Children's Society

"Give a child a happy heart –
adoption can make it happen"

The Catholic Children's Society is a well established voluntary adoption agency, which has found adoptive families for more than 2,000 children since its beginnings over 50 years ago. The Society believes that the experience of family life is crucial to the well being of all children and offers its adoption service to all children and families regardless of race or religious belief and practice.

The Society frequently acts as an advocate on behalf of adopted young people and uses every opportunity to ensure their views are heard. It believes that children and families are better served and empowered by the services the Society provides.

The Children's Society's

"If you believe every child deserves a decent chance in life,
you believe in everything we stand for"

The Children's Society's stated aim is to be a positive force for change in the lives of children and young people. The Society works to find new ways to discover the best in children who have experienced only the worst that life has to offer. It works with young teenagers held on remand in prison, providing accommodation and schooling. In schools, the Society works for children, parents and teachers to help get children who have truanted or been excluded back into the classroom.

On the streets the Society reaches out to child runaways and in prisons the aim is to turn around the lives of youngsters who have become involved in crime, and give them a fresh start.

The Society's promise is to be there for children as a friend, to care for them, to help them and to encourage them to achieve the potential that they all have.

Parents' Poetry

During the sixteen years Judy Theobald has been writing the weekly poetry column in the Lincolnshire Echo and Western Morning News, children have featured highly among her subject matter.

In this collection of verses, the trials of new babies, temperamental toddlers, stroppy seven-year-olds and angst-ridden adolescents are all set against that agonising moment when they leave home – and then come back again.

Her poems are politically very incorrect but writing them was a matter of, "survival in more ways than one," she says.

We ask for your prayers for all who have given service and dedicated their time to the furtherance of **The Catholic Children's Society** and **The Children's Society** over the years. This book is sponsored by the partners of O'Halloran & Company together with Judy Theobald, who donated the poetry. O'Halloran & Company is celebrating thirty years of providing family financial planning.

Judy Theobald's poetry may at times be irreverent but it is never irrelevant. It reflects the colourful montage that makes up life and all of the facets of family life in particular.

We all hope you enjoy this book and thank you for the support of the two charities that bring so much humour, joy, light, life and colour into many children's lives and the lives of those adults, parents, foster parents and adoptive parents whose lives the children touch.

Families are best because . . .

Of a cosy bed as snug as a nest
Grandmas who stay
Brothers who play
Sisters to help
Pets that yelp
Birthdays to share
Parents who care
Happy together
Sad together
Meals together
Fun together
Talk together
Laugh together
Love together
Stay forever.

Rosie, aged nine

CHILDREN!

Children! Who'd 'ave 'em?
It's not like the ads
With their smart fitted kitchens
And smug mums and dads.
It's quarrels and crying,
Being up half the night
And that terrible fear
You're not getting it right.

It's children not eating,
Not going to school,
And it's you in the middle
Not keeping your cool.
And it's feeling so weak
When your meant to be strong,
And everyone wondering
Where it went wrong.

But bring us those times
When you don't understand
Why it's all gone to pieces,
We'll lend you a hand;
Or those desperate days
When you're struggling to cope
With the tantrums and poverty,
We'll show you hope.

Bring us your runaway kids
Sleeping rough,
Or your children in prison
All trying to be tough
And pretend they don't care,
But we see from each face,
They are frightened and lonely
And in the wrong place.

Children! Who'd 'ave 'em?
We will, send them all,
The tearaways, bullied,
The large and the small.
And we will find joy
Where once there was sorrow.
Just bring us your children,
We'll give you tomorrow.

CHILDREN!

Pregnancy, ad nauseam

Sarah's feeling terrible
Whatever can it be?
She's feeling quite hungover
And yet all she's drunk is tea,
But her news is not that dreadful,
It's good, would you believe,
She's going have a baby
But right now, she's going to heave.

And everybody's overjoyed.
Come on, let's celebrate!
The champagne corks are popping
There are nibbles on the plate.
We shall toast the coming baby
But poor Sarah cries, "Be quick."
As she sips a glass of water
Then finds somewhere to be sick.

Pregnancy, ad nauseam

How cheerily the midwife says:
"It's not an illness dear,"
For Sarah it's been nine long months
Of coming over queer.
Of feeling there is nothing
She can eat at all on earth,
Then only stopping vomiting
In order to give birth.

As soon as it's all over
She lies sore and tired in bed,
Knowing everyone's gone out
To wet the baby's head.
Then she turns towards her baby
Lying precious, still and small.
Does it matter that she's felt so ill?
And she thinks: "No, not at all".

Lifestyles

"We won't let it alter our lifestyle a bit,"
They both say with steadfast intent
Announcing, with pleasure, to all of their friends
They're expecting a happy event.
"Small children should not disrupt anyone's life,
Should always be seen and not heard."
And of all of the people who listen to this
Not one of them dare say a word.

In due course, the infant appears on the scene,
And true, they've not slept for a week,
They can't sit and chat without baby in arms
But who cares, they can't hear themselves speak
Above all its screams. They haven't been out
As none of mum's clothes seem to fit,
But they're gritting their teeth and telling the world
It's not changed their lifestyle a bit.

Go back in two years and the house is all changed
For gone are the china and glass
Which once graced the sitting-room book case and
shelves,
Outside in the garden the grass
Has all disappeared under dollies and prams,
There's wellies and bikes in the hall,
And the talk is all potties and nursery schools
And they don't mention lifestyles at all.

A year on, they're all eating jelly for tea
Brought forward their bedtime to eight.
Their friends never call as they're in the same boat
And can't stay awake until late.
But they've wonderful news. They're soon to be joined
By a new little bundle of bounce,
And at least they can say with no word of a lie,
It won't change their lifestyle an ounce.

Lifestyles

Mum's mistake

When mum brought my new baby home
I knew I'd been deceived,
She promised it would play with me,
A promise I believed.
I planned some smashing cowboy games,
With lassoes all a whirl,
But boring baby slept all day
And worse, it was a girl.

My sister slept, my sister ate,
My sister screamed a lot.
To try to cheer her up
I put my football in her cot.
I filled it up with books and thought
She must be overjoyed,
But being a girl she only screamed
And mum just got annoyed.

She screamed, mum said, from hunger
Only then, what do you think,
Instead of having proper food
She just had stuff to drink.
So helpfully, I gave her crisps,
Some currant cake and bread
And then, instead of thanking me,
Mum sent me up to bed.

Mum's mistake

My baby sister grew a bit
And then she grew some more,
She reached my cupboards and my shelves,
She found my Lego drawer.
Mum says that having one of each
Has been her pride and joy.
Which shows just how much grown-ups know.
Next time, I want a boy.

BLAME IT ON THE FUTURE

Mrs McLaughlan's treasure,
Dear little, four-year-old Stan,
Discovered his mother's best scissors
And then, while she telephoned gran,
He cut all the fringe off the sofa,
And tastefully altered a hat,
Then, with a deft snip, produced a new breed,
Of rather surprised looking cat.

He cut down his mother's net curtains,
His sister was playing at brides,
And as the poor baby looked scruffy,
He gave it a short back and sides.
When mum finished talking to granny
And saw all the mess in the hall,
She couldn't believe that he'd chopped up so much
In the space of a telephone call.

When dad had a look at the damage
He threatened to leather his bum.
But mum, with an eye to the future,
Told dad what she thought of her son:
"He's really a budding Picasso,
So leave my poor Stanley alone."
Then she called round a couple of workmen
And got them to take out the phone.

Twenty years on and young Stanley,
His chopping-up instincts still keen,
Got a job in a government office,
Working their shredding machine.
And mum didn't mind in the slightest
At the absence of art on her walls,
For she'd managed three trips to Majorca,
On the saving in telephone calls.

BLAME IT ON THE FUTURE

In the dark

Each night when my mum
Comes to bid me goodnight
She kisses my forehead
And turns out the light.
Then she goes back downstairs
Leaving me in the gloom,
Alone with the monsters
That live in my room

I've a wolf in the wardrobe,
A bear on the stair
And it just doesn't help
When mum says they're not there.
She doesn't believe me
But I know for certain
A child-eating crocodile
Lives in my curtain.

And I'm not safe in bed
Because just underneath
Lives a black, green-eyed dog
With enormous sharp teeth,

All ready to grab
With his slavering jaw
If I dare to put
One of my toes on the floor.

There are lions on the landing
And snakes in the sink
So I dare not get up
If I fancy a drink.
And I lie there in terror
Sheets clamped round my chin
In case a stray tiger
Should try to climb in.

In the dark

Then come the next morning
The lovely bright sun
Has sent all the monsters
And beasts on the run.
And I just can't explain it,
I wish I did know
Exactly the place
Where those monsters all go.

Mothers' Day

Thank you so much for the breakfast,
I can't say what pleased me the most.
Was it the sauce on the cornflakes,
Or the lard which you spread on the toast?
And doesn't the coffee taste different
When the water comes straight from the tap.
But I know that you can't use the kettle,
You're still very young, little chap.

The brooch that you gave me is lovely;
Real emeralds spelling my name.
No, I don't think I know any ladies
Who own one exactly the same.
And thanks for the bottle of perfume,
It truly brought tears to my eyes.
I'm going to save it for summer
And use it to keep off the flies.

I think you're so clever, my darling,
To make such a beautiful card,
We should get the glue off the sofa
Though it seems to have set pretty hard.
Oh goodness. Is Dad cooking dinner?
I know that he's doing his best,
And I'm not for the minute complaining
But the smoke tends to get on my chest.

Thank heavens it's Monday tomorrow,
I'll spend the whole day on my feet
And polishing, scrubbing and scraping,
Clean up the effects of my treat.
It's not that I'm grumbling, my sweetheart,
Don't think I dislike it, my dear,
I'm just grateful that Mothering Sunday
Comes round only once every year.

Mothers' Day

"Come now, my little Jim, be brave,
Think how Britannia ruled the wave,
How she commanded sea and tide,
It wasn't by trembling at the side,
She set the oceans cowering
By waving her shield and pointy thing,
So copy Britannia, little Jim,
Be a good boy and learn to swim."

Swimming lessons

Between his mum and auntie Doreen
Jim stands fainting in the chlorine
Wafting from the pool below.
Swimmers' heads bob to and fro
As mum, with patience wearing thin,
Is just about to push him in,
Determined that her little son
Will join in all this happy fun.

But little Jim has other thoughts,
He doesn't fancy water sports.
Skinny in trunks, this little waif
Thinks indoor sports are far more safe,
Like postman's knock and tiddlywinks,
At least in Scrabble no-one sinks.
His mum can whistle Hearts of Oak,
He isn't going for a soak.

Swimming lessons

"Come on now, little Jim, be bold,
It's only momentarily cold,
Those waving arms and kicking legs
Will still those chattering toothipegs,
And listen to that screaming noise,
It's all the happy girls and boys,
So hurry up Jimmy, in you wade,
Besides which, darling, Mummy's paid."

THE BIRTHDAY PARTY

Happy birthday sweetheart,
You're six years old, I see,
And all your little schoolfriends
Are here today for tea.
I've sausages and sandwiches,
A cake that's like a train,
And I've got myself a double gin
In case I go insane.

A nasty gang of little boys
Is digging up the lawn,
And someone's pretty party frock
Has managed to get torn.
Meanwhile, a dozen footsteps
Are thumping overhead
And half a dozen bottoms
Are bouncing on my bed.

And tell me, who's the boy
Who said that Sarah was a toad?
She threw a violent tantrum
And has run off down the road,

And I know I ought to get her
And I know I should be quick,
But the child who won the bouncing game
Has managed to be sick.

When at last it's teatime
They stuff until they burst
And they hold a competition
As to who behaves the worst.
They grab at all the biscuits,
Gobble jellies by the ton,
So I'm pleased when I can tell them
That all of them have won.

I'm hiding in the kitchen
When the mums and dads arrive.
At least they can be grateful
That their child is still alive.
Then I gladly send them packing,
My conscience feeling clear
For I needn't have this agony
Until this time next year.

THE BIRTHDAY PARTY

FETE worse than death

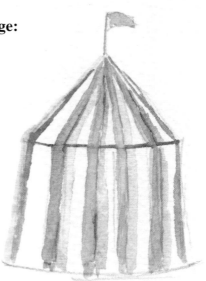

Bunting flutters round the playground
As the banner at the gate
Spreads the message to the village:
'June the 7th, Infants' Fete',
Promising cream teas, tombola,
Maypole dancing, yet again,
As the village population
Says its annual prayer for rain.

Everyone's been busy baking
Cakes embossed with sticky sweets,
In the tea tent tables groan
Beneath their high-cholesterol treats.
Children in their fancy dresses
All parade around the ring.
Beer tent does a roaring business
As the infants start to sing.

Mrs Sharpe, the school's headteacher,
Has the stall for bric-a-brac,
Mums, who cleared the house of rubbish,
Find they've paid to get it back.
Good old dad has bought some plants
Which promise him an evening spent
Not relaxing down the pub,
But over flower borders bent.

Time to make the thank-you speeches,
Hear the school's headteacher say
Months of frantic preparation
Went into this lovely day.
No-one dares to voice the question
Was it really worth it dear?
Spare us all this wanton fun
And let us send a cheque next year.

NEXT YEAR

PAY

Pets' corner

I have a little rabbit
And I love him very much
He lives out in my garden
In a cosy rabbit hutch.
He's more than just a pet to me
But a friend, I really need him.
But on the whole, I'd rather
Always let my mummy feed him.

My rabbit likes to scamper
All around the flower beds,
He nibbles all the leaves
And then eats all the tulip heads.
It's lovely when he's running
On the grass, so fresh and green,
Especially as it means that mum
Can give his hutch a clean.

When mummy went out shopping
We brought him in one day.
A sitting room's a lovely place
For bunnikins to play.
He nibbled through the phone wires,
Then, pricking up his ears,
Behind the sofa cushions
Left some little souvenirs.

He's such a funny bunny
That it came as a surprise
When mummy started talking
About casseroles and pies.
And she really was quite mean
To mention gloves made out of fur
When I wondered who I loved the most,
My bunnikins or her.

Pets' corner

The best messed room

Why does mum make me tidy up,
Why can't she be more lenient,
The way I've got my room set out
Is totally convenient.
I need my own untidiness,
I need my lovely mess,
My clothes heaped in a corner
Make it easier to dress.

I keep these empty cups and mugs
No matter what I'm told,
At present I'm conducting
Some experiments with mould.
And Lego's useless packed in sets,
It's meant to stay on floors,
And in case we get a hamster,
I keep all my apple cores.

How I wish my silly mother
Could get into her head
There's a very helpful filing system
Underneath my bed.
There's half a dozen library books,
A year's worth of the Dandy,
And if you want to find old socks
And vests it's very handy.

But parents are quite stupid
On account of being so old.
They say it's unhygienic
But you do not catch a cold
From sleeping in a bedroom
That's a lovely comfy mess.
Oh why does mum love tidiness,
Why can't she nag me less.

Holiday handicap

The runners are just about ready,
Today is the very first day
The School Summer Holiday Meeting
Has just about got under way.
They're all under starter's orders,
Straining to leave at the gate,
And then, with the final bell ringing,
They're all heading off down the straight.

Everyone's galloping freely,
Away on their holiday fun.
Yippee No School 'til September
Keeps up with In Bed Until One.
Farewell Old School Sweater is leading
Neck and neck with No Homework, Hooray!
But soon even he is being beaten
By Goody No English Today.

But there's trouble ahead for the runners,
The holiday heads for the jumps,
I'm Having A Great Time is beaten
By Bother My Friend's Got The Mumps,

Then, It's Not Fair is the leader,
With Everyone Else is Abroad,
Then finally, in comes the favourite,
That holiday winner, I'm Bored.

The race thunders on towards danger,
They've come to a terrible fence.
Tidy Your Bedroom has fallen,
But not, alas, Dreadful Expense.
And Day Tripper's coming through strongly,
Then after him, Beach, Sun and Sea,
Who tramples on Let's Do The Housework,
And Somebody Else Make the Tea.

Now everyone's running their fastest
The winning post hoves into sight.
The winner's I Don't Want to go Back to School,
Who was sired by A Good Dose of Fright.
But wait, there's a steward's decision,
The winner is one of the others,
It's Everyone's Back in the Classroom.
The number one favourite with mothers

Holiday handicap

DEFEETED

Imagine, for a moment,
This familiar little scene:
There's a woman in a shoeshop
With her daughter, aged thirteen.
Their mission is quite simple,
They are here today to choose
A sensible, well fitting
Pair of regulation shoes.

The mother is suggesting
That her little girl should try
A pair with pretty buckles
And perhaps a dainty tie,
And she sighs as she remembers
That when she was this age
Winkle-picker shoes with three-inch heels
Were all the rage.

Then the mother gasps in horror
As her daughter picks a pair
Not feminine, but more the type
The infantry would wear,

With soles as thick as tractor tyres
And yards of thick black laces,
And toecaps that will polish
To reflect her classmates' faces.

The mum says if she wants them
Then she isn't going to pay.
The daughter says she'll have to,
Whose feet are they anyway?
And haven't all her classmates
Got the self-same lovely pair,
But after all, her classmates
All have mums who really care.

The mother then capitulates,
She's feeling slightly miffed,
But not because of footwear,
More because she feels the rift
That says her daughter's growing up,
She's far too big to scold,
And almost imperceptibly,
Poor mum is growing old.

DEFEETED

Almost for ever

In her Beatrix Potter bedroom,
Teddy bears upon the bed
And the latest boy band poster
Leering down above her head,
Sally lies alone and weeping
On her soaking pillow case,
Bitter tears for Craig are falling
Down her adolescent face.

Was it not at school last Wednesday
By the open art room door,
Craig had held her hand in his hand,
Swore he'd love her ever more
With a passion true and loyal
Which lasted through to Friday tea,
Now he's sent a Valentine
To Susan Strickland from form three.

Dad is feeling quite bewildered,
Cannot understand his Sal,
Of the boyfriends he's encountered,
Craig's the most Neanderthal.

Mum at least does understand:
"She's known him since they both were seven.
There's more where he came from," she adds,
But does she know he came from heaven?

When at last it's time for Neighbours,
Sally pauses in her tears,
In an intellectual vacuum
Contemplates her empty years.
Will she stay unloved for ever,
Still alone at eighty-four?
Then her thoughts are interrupted,
Someone's knocking at the door.

Sally, rushing to the window
Spots a new admirer, Mike.
How she's always liked his hair,
The macho way he rides his bike.
Now she's wiping off the tearstains,
Calling greetings from above.
Soon he holds her hand in his hand,
Promises undying love.

Almost for ever

HORROR OF HORRORS

Aren't parents dreadful!
Oh, I loved them in my youth,
But when you're in your teens
You get to know the awful truth.
You have this awful paradox,
They're really out of touch,
Considering how old they are
They don't know very much.

Take fashion, for example,
My mother doesn't know
That leather shoes and denim jeans
Were never meant to go.
She still has pale-blue eyelids,
Does her lipstick in a pout,
My father wears a coat
That leaves his bottom sticking out.

My mother grumbles, loudly,
If she's short-changed in a shop.
My father's going bald
And combs his hair across the top.
In front of all my friends
My mum expected to be kissed.
Then, on my cousin's wedding day,
My father did the twist!

HORROR OF HORRORS

Aren't parents awful.
I pretend they're not with me,
Especially at McDonald's
When mum asks for Earl Grey tea.
Ideally, they'd both stay at home
If I could have my way,
But you really must put up with them -
Your parents have to pay.

The **odd** couple

Together they stand,
Such a quaint little pair,
One with black-lidded eyes
And her black rooted hair
Which is coloured in purple,
Streaked silver and blue,
In the side of her nose
Glints a diamond or two,
She has scarves round her neck
Little boots on her feet
And her skirt has a fringe
Which is scraping the street.

The other is dressed
In an elegant shirt,
A nice tailored jacket,
A smart pleated skirt.
No jewellery she wears
Except three rows of pearls,
Her grey hair is brushed
Into neat little curls.
Who would think as they look
At first one then the other,
These two ladies are, in fact
Daughter and mother.

The daughter looks down
At her mum's dowdy dress
And vows that she'll never
Turn into a mess.
The mother in turn
Feels it breaking her heart
That her nice little girl
Has turned into a tart.
But bravely through town
On their outing they go,
Each of them praying
They meet no one they know.

The **odd** couple

Fairground siren

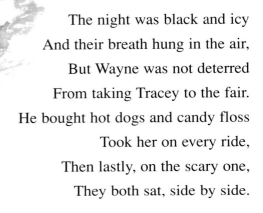

The night was black and icy
And their breath hung in the air,
But Wayne was not deterred
From taking Tracey to the fair.
He bought hot dogs and candy floss
Took her on every ride,
Then lastly, on the scary one,
They both sat, side by side.

With a wailing of the sirens,
And a trundling of its wheels,
And the beating of the music
And the frightened, girlish, squeals,
The ride began to thunder,
Light bulbs flashing green and red,
While Tracey's costly perm
Stuck at an angle to her head.

Then the car careered sideways,
Lurched around and spun again,
Whirling Tracey like a dervish
'Til she turned and clutched at Wayne,
And the knowledge tingled through him,
How his friends would be impressed
When they heard the sixth-form siren
Nestled close into his chest.

Fairground siren

The music, and Wayne's pulse
Kept up a steady, fairground beat,
The ride came to an end
And Tracey staggered to her feet.
Wayne smirked; she still clung on,
This final fright had done the trick,
Then he turned to watch his sweetheart
Being violently sick.

It's a steal

The house has just exploded into uproar,

Today, it is the first day back at school,

The children have erupted into frenzy,

While you just stand there, trying to keep your cool,

For they are trying to grapple with a problem,

A problem which you think defies belief,

For since the time they broke up and this morning,

You've had the most peculiar kind of thief.

He didn't take the microwave or telly,

The silver still sits safely in its drawers,

In fact, you feel a little bit insulted,

He didn't take a single thing of yours.

Instead he only robbed the children's bedrooms,

Took everything they needed for today,

For, as they can't find uniforms or school books,

They say a thief has stolen them away.

Oh children, I am certain at this moment,
Our thief's negotiating with a fence,
Together they are reading 'French for Fourth Years',
Translated verbs into the present tense.
Maybe the thief has laid your 'Fun With Physics'
Before the fence's avaricious eyes,
Perhaps they're up some alleyway discussing
The current market price in 'hot' school ties.

It's a steal

Considering your serious allegations
Why don't you let me call the CID?
Or do you think we might just find the answer
If both your rooms were searched once more, by me,
When goodness, how surprising, I've discovered
That everything you need is on the floor.
The thief has brought them back when we weren't looking
And you can both return to school once more.

A thank-you note

Thank you, thank you Mr Smart,
You, who taught my children art,
Told them that they should explore a
Whole variety of flora.
Driftwood, sealife from the shore
Were spread in heaps upon the floor.
But though they drew their pictures well
They couldn't reproduce the smell.

Thank you, thank you Miss McPhee
Who taught my kids geography.
They had to find the origins
Of all the food that comes in tins,
By separating tin from label
They discovered they were able
To achieve this, except we
Were eating pears on toast for tea.

Grateful thanks to Mrs Burke
Who taught my children needlework.
The article, a pencil case,
Took yards of fabric, zip and lace,
A term to stitch then, what bad luck,
We filled it and the zip got stuck,
And with the contents thus encased
The whole lot had to be replaced.

$3 \times 3 =$

$6x \times 4y =$

$3y \times 2x =$

A thank-you note

Thank you, thank you Mr Benn
Who taught them, by the age of ten
Sufficient maths to make me look
As though I'd never read a book,
And couldn't count or read, or spell,
Alas you did it far too well
Dear teachers, you have done the trick,
The kids look clever, I look thick.

Morning has broken

Morning has broken,
Hark to it crashing,
Overhead footsteps
Vibrate the floor,
Drawers are dragged open,
Wardrobe doors shudder,
Radio One fights
Radio Four.

Down they all thunder
Fresh from their slumber
Groaning: "Why must this
Happen to me?
Life is just torture,
Mornings are murder."
Under your breath you
Quietly agree.

"Where are my school clothes?
Didn't I hang them,
Safe in my room
The evening before?"

See in the night
They've been on a wander,
Found a new hanger
Down on the floor.

Smouldering hair tongs
Singeing the sofa,
Up in the bathroom hear the taps run,
Twenty-five minutes
Spent on the hairstyle,
See the disaster
When it's all done.

Mornings are peaceful
When they've departed,
Silence and order
Fill the house then.
Such is the trauma
Of these dawn risings,
Why can't the day start
Nearer to ten?

Morning has broken

Hush dear, the world might hear you

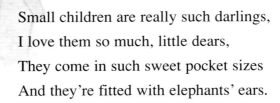

Small children are really such darlings,
I love them so much, little dears,
They come in such sweet pocket sizes
And they're fitted with elephants' ears.

But you'll never find hatred or malice
Residing within their small souls,
They haven't a horrible thought in their minds,
And they haven't got volume controls.

So combine what they hear in each elephant ear
With the tannoy they've got in their head,
And the people who live at the corner find out
You're quite glad that their goldfish dropped dead.

And little girls love to go shopping,
Especially for clothes, with their mother,
And look at their eyes, when they broadcast your size
From one end of the shop to the other.

And the butcher hears, sweetly, that mum said
You can resole your shoes with his ham,
And granny goes red when she hears that you said
She's just mutton all dressed up as lamb.

Hush dear, the world might hear you

But a child is a lovely companion,
A comfort until your life ends,
Which is just as well, when you consider
By then you'll have lost all your friends.

No kidding

I won't even mention the labour pains
Or the sickness that came before,
I'm not going to talk of the pram in the hall
And the way that it blocked the front door.
I'm not going to say the words: "Broken nights"
All those years when you fought with sleep,
Nor will I grumble about the toys,
The bikes and the planes and stuffed sheep.

For didn't I think when you went to school
Life would get suddenly easy,
But I forgot about tummy aches, rashes and colds,
And fevers and kids feeling queasy.
And never once did I anticipate
The times I'd be summoned to go
Down to the school to say to the head:
"He's really a nice boy, you know."

No kidding

Then came the dreaded teenage years,
Full of exams and doubt,
Of kids lounging around in the house all the day
Or otherwise always being out.
And kids, when they're led to an ironing board
Suddenly losing control,
And never learning to switch off a light,
Or cope with a washing-up bowl.

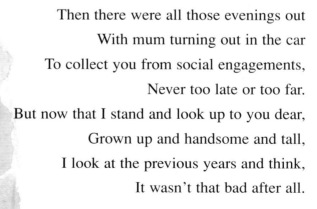

Then there were all those evenings out
With mum turning out in the car
To collect you from social engagements,
Never too late or too far.
But now that I stand and look up to you dear,
Grown up and handsome and tall,
I look at the previous years and think,
It wasn't that bad after all.

Goodbye

And now it's time to say goodbye,
I won't embarrass you and cry.
Nearby another mum and dad
Are trying to pretend they're glad
Their grown-up child has left the nest
And even though we do our best
It's obvious to all who see
We're shrouded in anxiety.

You've passed the academic stuff
But do you really know enough
About the things that really count
Like bus routes, and the right amount
Of cash to live on. Please beware
Of pickpockets and do take care
When out alone at night, and try
To keep your socks and footwear dry.

And did I mention, did I say,
You must eat three square meals a day?
Short years ago I wouldn't let
You cross the road alone and yet,
You're off now, independently,
To live a life away from me,
For fate has given you a shove
Away from my protective love.

And will the love that you have known
Stand by you now you're on your own?
And why, when you can fill our hall
At home, you now look very small
Outside your university,
Two hundred miles from home, and me.
It's really time to say goodbye.
I'm sorry dear. I'll have to cry.

Goodbye

The empty house

They'd gone, and back at home you found
A Noddy cup, and wept.
But later, the first night for months
You went to bed and slept.
Next morning, when you went to fetch
The scissors from the drawer,
You found them, and the room looked
As it had the night before.

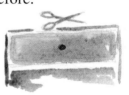

In the bathroom, your conditioner
Was still there, on the shelf.
You bathed, and used up gallons
Of hot water on yourself.
You found a playgroup photograph
And had a little cry.
But enjoyed the lack of washing
Hanging on the line to dry.

That first week, guilt assailed you.
"I must rush home," you said.
But with nothing to rush home to
You stayed having fun instead.
You lay in bed at weekends
With the pleasing thought in mind
That when you finally got up
There'd be no mess to find.

You missed their noise and laughter
Buying treats for them in shops.
But you didn't miss the food bill
Or the dire Top of the Pops.
And you didn't miss preparing meals
To watch them sit and moan.
And then they phoned you up and said:
"Hi mum, we're coming home!"

The empty house

Changing times

You have coaxed it to eat its cabbage
But lived eighteen years on peas,
You've protected it from winter's cold
And summer's stinging bees,
You have always aired its bed well,
And made sure its clothes are dry,
You've given it cash when needed
And a shoulder on which to cry.

You listened to every problem,
Wiped away all the tears,
Gave it what wisdom you'd gathered,
Over the long, tough years.
You have steered it, you think, successfully,
Away from the imprudent,
But suddenly, all that's disappeared,
The child's become a student.

And it's living on pasta and pizza,
Cold baked beans and tepid beer,
And its music is loud enough for folk
A mile away to hear.
And it's getting bits of its body pierced
And even more bits of its head,
And it's so long since its sheets were washed,
They're crackling on the bed.

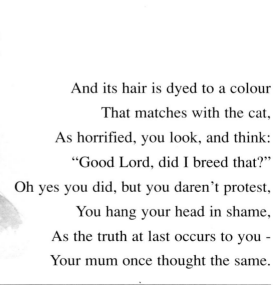

And its hair is dyed to a colour
That matches with the cat,
As horrified, you look, and think:
"Good Lord, did I breed that?"
Oh yes you did, but you daren't protest,
You hang your head in shame,
As the truth at last occurs to you -
Your mum once thought the same.

Two's company

I'll mind the twins, I said,
What could be easier?
Medically, this is what's known
As amnesia.
I had two babies,
A sister and brother,
But they kindly got here,
One after the other.
Twins, just like buses,
Get there in twos,
And when you've a crisis,
Which one do you choose?

I'd imagined the babies
Would sleep in their prams,
But the twins, I discovered,
Had made other plans.
They wanted a bottle,
Then they wanted a walk,
And when we got home
They both wanted a talk.
They fancied a biscuit
Then cried for their tea,
Then they both sneezed and sprayed it
All back over me.

And they dribbled, like waterfalls,
All down their chests
Till it soaked through their jumpers,
And drenched both their vests,
So I whipped off their clothes
And then found, what a pain,
They were too small and fiddly
To get dressed again.
Even worse, when I got them
To lie flat for me,
I turned, and they both rolled
Beneath my settee.

Bathtime. I forgot
How a small infant feels
When it's covered with soap,
It's like slithering eels.
But I sloshed them both round
In the warm sudsy water
Then mummy arrived to find
Each little daughter
Clean, fit and well.
"Did you manage?" she cried.
I have to confess, at this juncture,
I lied.

Two's company

Age-old problems

She's nearly three, she's very cross
She wants you all to know she's boss
Your very tiniest request
Is treated as the greatest test
She never stands when asked, or sits
But does the opposite and spits
As though she's in a dreadful rage
But never mind, it's just her age.

She's seventeen, life isn't fair,
She's got the most revolting hair
Her face is fat, her teeth are large,
Her bottom's bigger than a barge.
Each day she rants that life is mean
To someone who is just a teen
And cannot earn a decent wage,
But never mind, it's just her age.

She's fifty-three, life's passed her by,
She notices, with downcast eye
Her hair is grey, her face is lined
And worse than that she cannot find
Her handbag or her front door key,
She's lost her short-term memory.
Nor can she see to read a page,
But never mind, it's just her age.

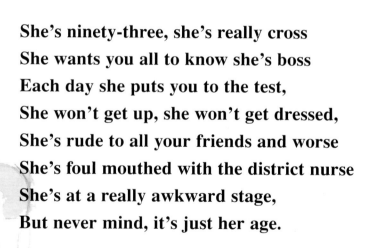

She's ninety-three, she's really cross
She wants you all to know she's boss
Each day she puts you to the test,
She won't get up, she won't get dressed,
She's rude to all your friends and worse
She's foul mouthed with the district nurse
She's at a really awkward stage,
But never mind, it's just her age.

Age-old problems

Regional Offices

Catholic Children's Society

Mrs M.Dight
Catholic Children's Society, 7 Colwick Road, West Bridgford, Nottingham NG2 5FR
Mary Gandy
CCWC, St Joseph's Centre, Watford Way, Hendon, London NW4 4TY
Mr T.Connor
Catholic Children's Society, Arundel & Brighton, 49 Russell Hill Road, Purley CR8 2XB
Mr J.Richards
CCS Westminster, 73 St Charles Square, London W10 6EJ
Mr G.Edwards
Catholic Children's Society Shrewsbury, St Paul's House, Farmfield Drive, Greenfields, Beechwood, Birkenhead L43 7ZT
Mrs B.Warwick
East Anglia Diocesan Children's Society, C/o 4 Mason Road, Swanton Morley, Dereham NR20 4NN
Mr S.Small
St Andrew's Children's Society, Gillis Centre, 113 Whitehouse Loan, Edinburgh EH9 1BB
Ms M.Campbell
St Margaret's Children & Family Care Society, 274 Bath Street, Glasgow, G2 4JR
Ms P.McGrogan
Family Care Society, 511 Ormeau Road, Belfast BT7 3GS
Ms A.Forbes
Catholic Agency for Social Concern, 39 Eccleston Square, London SW1V 1BX
Mr S.Hanlon
Catholic Care, St Paul's, 11 North Grange Road, Leeds LS6 2BR
Rev Fr T.Dougherty
Catholic Child Care, Diocese of Middlesbrough, Curial Offices, 50a The Avenue, Linthorpe, Middlesbrough RS5 6QT
Mr K.Caffrey
Father Hudson's Society, Coventry Road, Coleshill, Birmingham B46 3ED
Mr B.Stone
Hallam Diocesan Caring Service, St Wilfrid's Centre, 524 Queen's Road, Sheffield S2 4DT
Mr A.Harrison
St Francis Children's Society, Collis House, 48 Newport Road, Woolstone, Milton Keynes MK15 0AA
Mr F.Maguire
Brentwood Catholic Children's Society, "Fairview", 77 Queens Road, Brentwood, Essex CM14 4HD
Mr G.Cooney
Catholic Children and Family Care Society, Bishop Brown House, Durham Street, Grangetown, Cardiff CF1 7PB
Mrs J.Ball
Catholic Children's Society (Clifton), 58 Alma Road, Clifton, Bristol, BS8 2DQ
Mr A.Donohoe
St Cuthberts Care, St Cuthbert's House, West Road, Newcastle-Upon-Tyne NE15 7PY
Mr J.Cullen
Catholic Caring Services, 218 Tulketh Road, Ashton-on-Ribble, Preston PR2 1ES
Mr J.Kennedy
The Nugent Care Society, 150 Brownlow Hill, Liverpool, L3 5RF
Mrs C.Davis
Plymouth Diocesan CCS Ltd, C/o Exeter Diocesan Board for Christian Care, Glenn House, 96 Tiverton Road, Exeter EX4 6LD
Rev Fr B.Wilson
Catholic Children's Rescue Society Salford, 390 Parrs Wood Road, Manchester M20 5NA

The Children's Society

East of England
The Children's Society, 20-2 White House Road, Alpha Business Park, Ipswich, Suffolk 1PI 5LT
North
The Children's society, 3rd Floor, Stamford House, Picadilly, York YO1 9PW
South East
The Children's Society, 91-93 Queens Road, Peckham, London SE15 2EZ
South West
The Children's Society, Brrok House, Pennywell Road, Bristol, BS5 0TX
West
The Children's Society, Unit4, Mitre Court, Lichfield Road, Sutton Coalfield, West Midlands B74 2LZ
Wales
The Children's Society, 14 Cathedral Road, Cardiff, CF11 9LI